Lessons from a Quilt

LESSONS FROM A
QUILT

AMY LEVESQUE

XULON PRESS

Xulon Press
2301 Lucien Way #415
Maitland, FL 32751
407.339.4217
www.xulonpress.com

© 2021 by Amy Levesque

All rights reserved solely by the author. The author guarantees all contents are original and do not infringe upon the legal rights of any other person or work. No part of this book may be reproduced in any form without the permission of the author. The views expressed in this book are not necessarily those of the publisher.

Due to the changing nature of the Internet, if there are any web addresses, links, or URLs included in this manuscript, these may have been altered and may no longer be accessible. The views and opinions shared in this book belong solely to the author and do not necessarily reflect those of the publisher. The publisher therefore disclaims responsibility for the views or opinions expressed within the work.

Paperback ISBN-13: 978-1-6628-3836-1
Ebook ISBN-13: 978-1-6628-3837-8

Table of Contents

Introduction ix

Part 1: *Trials and Tribulations* 1
Chapter 1 3
Chapter 2 5
Chapter 3 7
Chapter 4 11
Chapter 5 13
Chapter 6 17
Chapter 7 21
Chapter 8 25
Chapter 9 29
Chapter 10 33
Chapter 11 37
Chapter 12 39

Part 2: *Lessons from a Quilt* 45
Chapter 13 47
Chapter 14 49
Chapter 15 55
Chapter 16 61
Chapter 17 65
Chapter 18 69

Acknowledgements 71

Introduction

What you are about to read is not the initial version I had intended. Sure, the message is the same, but the way of telling it is quite different. The original idea was to write a fictional story, completely devoid of my own situation, but with the same result. That story did begin to come to life, but I got restless with it. I didn't know why, but I just didn't want to continue it. I prayed over it every day for a week, and during one of my morning "clear my head" runs, the reason was provided.

I was attempting to tell the story, but at no risk to myself. By that, I simply mean that I was ensuring that my own faults would remain sealed away, and therefore, I would not be made vulnerable. At that moment, it was clear that for the message to be truly as intended, I had to show myself. My emotions, struggles, and all that came with it had to be exposed. I was meant to tell MY story, just as you are meant to tell yours. It was a scary prospect, but one that I realize is vital and necessary to the message I hope you receive. By sharing myself and some of my story, I hope to help someone else. I do not claim to have all the answers; in fact, I have probably very few. What I do present here is how I personally have, through hard lessons and renewed faith, been an overcomer. These lessons that began over twenty-five years ago with a simple analogy, are now words of encouragement I offer to you. It is my hope that you can find something of value here. Although we may never meet, my prayer is that you find some strength, peace, and your own path toward faith.

This book is designed as a quick read. The first part is simply to tell some parts of my own story, as abridged as possible. The second gives the lessons of the quilt in a practical way and with simple takeaways that, when applied, can help you exercise your faith and grow in ways that you never thought possible.

Part 1
Trials and Tribulations

Chapter 1

How far back do I go to start this journey with you? I guess a quick snapshot of my faith growing up is necessary, so that the path I have traveled will make sense somehow. My parents divorced when I was a baby. I have no memories of us as a family unit... not one. Several years ago, I was given three or four pictures of the three of us, which I safely keep as a reminder that we were, at one time, a family. Growing up, I divided my time between the two households. Both of my parents remarried when I was under the age of 2 and added half-sisters to the dynamic. I lived mainly with my mother and spent every other weekend with my dad. It was just the way things were.

I remember a handful of times when I attended church with my dad, but at my mother's house we were very involved in the church. My stepfather was both youth and music minister, and so we were at church every time the doors were open. I sang in the church choir, and as a soloist. We even traveled to other churches to perform, as he was in a quartet as well. Amy Grant's song *My Father's Eyes* was my first solo, and I still remember it to this day. I strived to live in my Christian walk. I certainly wasn't perfect by any means, no human can be, but I tried. I was independent and a little rebellious. I even remember once being punished by having to write the commandment about honoring your father and mother 100 times. I can still quote it in full today! Still, some of my best memories of my youth were from the summer youth camps and various church activities I was so frequently part of.

I tell you all of this to lay the groundwork that I had a strong faith growing up. I aspired to be a Christian singer. So how does a person go from wanting to serve, to questioning God and faith? What makes a person turn away and look for answers on their own? Can one even find their way back? What happens when you finally get your answers? There are many different answers depending on your own circumstances. The lessons of the quilt are the answers for me. Maybe one or all of them can be answers for you as well.

Chapter 2

My first real wayward steps happened in the teenage years. The second family I had come to be part of with my mother somehow fell apart, and now I found myself with my mother and sister in a small apartment. My mother slept on the couch so that we could have our own rooms. It was such a small gesture, but it was something about her that has stayed with me through the years. She wanted to keep our lives as normal as possible, and she went without at times so that we could have what we needed. Sadly, this is something I repeated with my own children years later when I would struggle to support the three of us.

For me, I couldn't understand what happened. They had said so many times at church that families built around faith were stronger, and yet here we were, broken again. It was the first time that I found myself questioning what I was being taught. With the marriage dissolved, we no longer even attended the church that we had been such an integral part of for years. In one slam of the gavel, their marriage, and my connection to the church and my friends there, were gone. Oh, we tried to go back, but there was a sense of not belonging. This made me question the church too. Weren't we supposed to accept everyone without judgment?

I now know that even churches, as symbols of love and acceptance, are still made up of people. People are the ones that let us down, not God. We did try other churches, and though I don't really remember exactly when, eventually we stopped going. My mother still got up every morning at 4:00 AM to read her Bible and pray. I, however, fell into some of the temptations of youth. I became rebellious and independent in my thinking. I wanted to have my faith restored and would question my mother about why things happened the way they did. Her primary answer to me, for every situation was, "Everything happens for a reason."

Chapter 3

Everything happens for a reason.

These words were almost always spoken by my mother in times of disappointment. They echoed in my head, even into my adulthood. The mantra was somehow supposed to make things better, but mostly filled me with frustration, and sometimes anger. I had indulged her over the years with a hardened smile and false acceptance that yes, everything did happen for a reason.

"We may not always understand the reason, but there is one, nonetheless. God knows the reason," my mother would say. That was her way of trying to make sense of whatever situation plagued me, while knowing that I did not abide by the same understanding.

Not getting the part I wanted in a school play, the ebb and flow of friends, missed opportunities, being passed over for promotions, and even a broken heart. All these could be explained away with one simple, unadorned sentence. *Everything happens for a reason.* The next few years set the stage for me to enter the realm of explanation, though not fully into true understanding. It took many more years and heartaches for that to occur.

In my junior year of high school, I came home one day to my mother's boyfriend sitting in the living room. This was out of normal routine because I was always home before my mother, who was a seamstress by trade. Immediately, I wanted to know why he was there. His simple reply was, "I live here now. We're married."

Internally, I was in a full-blown rage. I was furious that my mother would simply take a day off work and go get married without even mentioning it to me. I mean, what mother does that?

In full self-reflection years later, I could admit that I had a definite attitude towards him from that point on. Now older and at least a little wiser, I believed it was because, for several years, it had just been me and mom. When he joined the picture, I didn't like losing her attention, especially since my dad and I weren't particularly close at this time.

Again, in retrospect, I didn't want to give up my time with friends on the weekend to visit him, when I had no friends there. It was a bit of selfish behavior on my part, but when you are a teenager, isn't that the way of things? I sometimes felt that I was an outsider in his new family, which created tension at that age. There were also things behind the scenes that contributed that I didn't know about until many years later, when we began to talk and try to salvage a relationship between us. Only in the past couple of years have we been able to see that each of us were feeling the same emotions but from opposite sides of the picture. It

Chapter 3

is still my prayer that we can close the past and focus on the future that we still have together. Life is short and should not be wasted on things that cannot be changed. Focus on the positives and build from there.

Back to the story at hand…a couple of years later, upon my graduation from high school, I was told by my mother to find somewhere else to live because of all the tension between my stepfather and me. Going to my father's was not an option so I had to figure something out. They did help me of course by giving me a set of luggage as a graduation gift.

Chapter 4

In an interesting twist, I lived with my ex-stepfather for a while after graduation, and then with my best friend. You could probably see what's coming next. I wish I had been able to, but hindsight, as they say, is 20/20. I married at 19. Far too young and for all the wrong reasons. At the first opportunity to feel like I had a place to really belong, with someone who professed to love me and wanted to give me all my dreams, I went straight into the deep end of the pool. There were warning signs early on, but I ignored them because I wanted stability in any form.

Faith for me was part of my past, safely tucked away in the depths of my consciousness. I knew it existed but had no desire to practice it. I wish I could tell you why I felt that way, but I simply cannot pinpoint a specific reason. My husband did not really practice religion and to go anywhere without him was not part of his plan. Bibles were packed away and only my conversations with my mother would provide any sort of faith-based undertone. Most of these conversations were with me under duress with something not working out the way I wanted it to. Always, her answer was that God loved me and that, as you probably guessed, *Everything happens for a reason.*

It should shock no one that I found myself where I did and with the eventual outcome. For the protection of everyone, I won't divulge specifics of the marriage except where necessary. Ultimately, there were moments of both emotional and physical abuse, and unfaithfulness, that I will reserve for another day. What you should know is that eventually, aside from my mother, I really had no friends and no lifelines to reach out to. I was completely sequestered from everyone and everything, faith included. Completely immersed in a world of control and manipulation I was unable to realize was happening until many years later. Faith ultimately freed me from that life, and was in fact, the only thing. For the purposes of this book, I will save those stories for future discussion.

Chapter 5

The year after we married, I was expecting our first child. While working at my second job, one day I had terrible cramping and discovered blood running down my leg. I knew enough to realize that, at only six weeks pregnant, this was bad. Immediately, I was taken to the hospital and after the examination, I was told that it was a near miscarriage. The doctors advised me to consider terminating the pregnancy and gave me two weeks of bed rest to ponder the suggestion, and to see if things would be okay, though they felt otherwise.

I found myself reaching into the innermost parts of my heart and dusting off my faith. Isn't that the way we typically act? When things are good, we don't seem to require our faith; however, the very instant things turn for the worse, it is where we often go. We ask for forgiveness first, for help second, and then, if our prayers are answered, we return our faith back to the pantry for future use. Okay, maybe not everyone does it that way, but I sure have. Don't feel bad if you also recognize yourself in that statement. More of us do that than don't. It's called being human.

During that time, I did begin to pray and to seek answers. I would love to say that I humbled myself before God, but that would be untrue. It began with a question to Him: Why? I wanted to be told why my baby was at risk and why I would, quite possibly, be robbed of the gift I had been given. It was unfair and I could not accept that God would do things that were hurtful. Hadn't I been told my entire young life about His love for me? This did not feel like love at all; it felt like punishment.

My mother came to sit with me and brought me a quilt she had made for me. (Once I had moved out of the house, the tension between everyone seemed to subside.) I covered up with that quilt constantly, sometimes for comfort more than warmth. During this time, I saw two forms of faith. Hers, which was so trusting and accepting of what the outcome might be. Mine was fraught with questions, requests, frustrations, and even promises that if my pregnancy would survive, I would be faithful to Him again. I ventured to guess that we could all find ourselves in at least one of those forms of faith, probably more the second. The good news is that God did answer my prayers. My son was born healthy, though the pregnancy was extremely difficult, and labor even more so. I, however, failed God once again and as soon as life was back to routine, I jarred my faith for another day. It wasn't that I didn't want to keep my promises to Him. I was alone in doing so, and it became easier to go with the rest of the people in our circle than risk being ridiculed or left out of the social circles in which we were accustomed. I am embarrassed now to even say that I

Chapter 5

was worried about what people might think of me if I led with my faith, but then again, so was Judas, and Jesus still loved him.

Chapter 6

The quilt my mother made for me became "The Quilt" in our home. If you were sick, the quilt was the last piece of the cure. When you were sad about anything, the quilt somehow gave you a sense of comfort and feeling that it would all be okay. Eventually for me, during the lonely days, it made me feel like I was not alone. I always said it was my momma in that quilt holding me close, but I now know that it was God. God was there for me, even when I didn't recognize it. Momma made it with love, and so part of her was definitely in it, but that quilt came to represent so much more. It was the very thing to help me through some of the darkest points of my life. It would also serve as the representation of faith that I still hold to this very day.

There are moments in life that define us, change us, break us, or propel us forward. July 8, 1995, marked me forever and brought my journey in and out of faith from the depths of my heart to what seemed like a battlefield. That morning, I was leaving for the store and, in usual fashion, my mother yelled down to me from her window. We lived literally just a driveway apart, and so we would often talk from window to window for quick moments. It was a beautiful summer day and they were going to go for a motorcycle ride. I was seven months pregnant with my second child and feeling the effects of swollen feet and hands due to the heat of summer. I wanted to be anywhere with air conditioning. She was excited and said they would be back by dinner. My husband, at the time, was working a second job in the evenings and was scheduled to work, so I had decided to just eat with them when they got back. I went about my day and around 3:00 PM, my son and I took a nap. When I woke up around 5:00 PM, I looked outside, but didn't see them back yet. At 7:00 PM, I was a little concerned that I hadn't heard anything. We were supposed to have dinner, and normally if they changed plans she would let me know. I made a quick dinner for my son and I, and as it started to get darker, I turned on the TV, expecting to hear the roar of the motorcycle engine in the driveway at any moment.

It is amazing what remains in our memory from moments like this. I can remember even the tiniest of details. I was watching the TV show *Walker, Texas Ranger*, which my mom had gotten me hooked on. I saw lights coming up the driveway, but not the sound I expected. It was also too early for my husband to be coming home. Before I even went to the door, I already knew. I felt sick and I didn't open the door. I stood in my kitchen, staring at the door while the police officer and my stepfather's sister let themselves in. I looked at them and simply said, "Is she dead?"

Chapter 6

She reached for me. I screamed and fell on my knees to the floor. Immediately, the battle with my faith raged inside me. "Why God? Why her? Why would you let this happen?" Only silence came.

Chapter 7

I took the quilt with me as we went to join my stepfather's family who had gathered at his mother's home. Walking in the door, I met the most surreal moment. It felt like in a movie scene where the main character was standing still and in focus, but all around them was just noise and blurry scenes. People talked, hugged me, and tried to get me to sit down or eat, or asked how I was doing. What a completely ridiculous question to ask! How did they expect me to be doing? I didn't answer or return any comments to anyone. I did, however, focus on my stepfather, alive, sitting on the couch opposite my chair. My stomach felt like I had just downed a glass of curdled milk. At that moment, I was angrier than I could ever remember being in my whole twenty-three years of existence. He sat there, some scrapes and bruises, but very much alive. How could that possibly be? Scrapes and bruises would heal, but my mother was dead. The thought that I would never see her again was more than I could stand. I had to get out of that place, away from him. It was as if, in that moment, he became the visual reminder of how unfair life could truly be. It also pushed me to question God even further. I was so angry.

My husband and I left and drove the forty-five minutes to my grandmother's home. At least there I would be surrounded by my mother's family. Maybe it would help me feel that she wasn't really gone. All the way there, I just kept asking God "why?" The more I tried to reason it in my own mind, the worse it got. Why would someone who had been so faithful to Him and so giving to others be taken away while my stepfather continued to live. It was so unfair, and I was overcome by bitterness, resentment, and anger toward my stepfather; and I hate to admit it now, even toward God.

Arriving at my grandmother's house was less overwhelming, but the pain didn't subside. A change of scenery doesn't make your internal problems go away. You have to face it head on, but I wasn't ready. At that moment, the problem was with God and His decision to take my mother when I needed her most in my life. Here I was about to give birth to my second child, with a toddler already, and also suspicious of my husband's faithfulness. She was helping me with all of it. Just two days before, we had gone to my OB/GYN appointment and heard the baby's heartbeat. She was so excited for her new grandbaby to be born. She couldn't wait to hold her, but that day would never come. I was later focused on one thing that kept rolling in my head. How cruel could He be to take her now? Her work wasn't finished here; I needed her more than He did. Someone said those famous words to me... *Everything happens for a reason*. I was furious. There was absolutely no reason for this,

Chapter 7

and no one could convince me otherwise. On the outside, I kept a calm and stoic face. My turmoil was purely on the inside. If there was one thing my mother had taught me, it was to keep it together and be strong for everyone else. If ever there was a test of my ability, it was now. I'm happy to say I excelled.

Chapter 8

Over the next few days, there were funeral plans to be made. I had a wall around me and my emotions were so high that even Goliath couldn't get through. Don't get me wrong here, I cried. A lot. I tried to do it in private as much as possible. I was asked to take charge of some of the planning. I took care of the flowers for her casket, the obituaries for the newspapers, and even selected the dress she would be buried in. It was a white two-piece, silky jacket and skirt. It was her favorite and, to me, she looked like the angel I knew she now was. The music for her service was also mine to organize. Sadly, we have had some losses in our family and it seemed that two songs were almost like standard funeral songs for our family. Anthems, if you will. "Go Rest High on that Mountain" was one. The other was a version of "Amazing Grace," sung by me. It was my mother's favorite hymn and she loved how I sang it. How ironic that I would have to sing about grace and being saved when I was feeling so angry, and even doubtful, of God's love. I knew I could never sing it live because my strong facade would most certainly turn to dust. I decided to pre-record it. I also recorded myself singing, "Eagle When She Flies," which, in my opinion, was the perfect description of my mother. To this day, I am unable to hear any of these songs and not flash back to this time in my life. Now, however, I have a different view on things. If there is one thing I do know for certain, God is very, very patient. We should all be thankful that He is!

The day came to receive friends at the funeral home and I was doing everything I could to keep it together. Every time someone would say to me that mom was happy with God now, I would smile and agree on the outside. On the inside, my eyes were rolling, and my indifference toward God was swelling. She was happy here, so I didn't see the point for God to take her away. My doctor was concerned that the stress would put me into early labor, so they had given me medication to have on hand, just in case. They were suggesting that I do some therapy, but the only person I wanted answers from was God, and He wasn't responding.

We arrived at the funeral home two hours before the visitation so that we could have our own private time with mom. The director said that there had already been a few people who came by to sign the book. I looked at the names. There were five or six names, but one in particular hit me like an eighteen-wheeler head on. It was my father. We hadn't spoken in several years, yet here was his name. He had been to the funeral home when I wasn't there. I was angry about it. There wasn't much I wasn't angry about during this time. This time my anger had an accomplice. Hurt was the silent partner that I was trying to ignore. When I saw that name,

Chapter 8

it was the first time that hurt bubbled to the surface and overtook every other emotion. Even though we hadn't spoken in about five years, I was hurt that he would not be there for me during this time, but that he would pay his respects from a distance. I stood there for several minutes trying to understand. Did he really dislike me so much that he couldn't put the issues aside for a time like this? I tried to reason it all out and to figure out why he would even have come at all, but nothing made sense. Was it a sense of obligation to her as my mother? Was it his way of letting me know that he knew what had happened? Was he trying to show me support? A name on a page wasn't what I needed. Truthfully, I didn't know what I needed, but looking back on it now, God knew. He always knew. He made sure I would get it too, in His timing.

Chapter 9

The public visitation hours were exhausting and a complete blur. Because I was seven months pregnant, everyone was swarming around me to make sure I was okay. I remember glasses of water and people telling me to just sit and take it easy. I appreciated the concern, but what I remembered most is feeling numb. It was as if my mind clicked off, a survival mechanism, I suppose, and the visitation hours were only fragments in my mind. Activity and voices swirled around me like the whipping wind of a hurricane. We extended visitation hours by almost two hours because of the amount of people coming to pay their respects. At the end, the funeral director discussed that he did not think the chapel would hold the amount of people who may attend the service, and so we agreed to move the service to the church that she had been attending, and that many of my family were a part of as well. I remembered standing at her casket, looking at her, and seeing only some small bruises on her hands. Nothing that would indicate such a severe outcome. She did look peaceful, and almost every person said how she was now happy in Heaven with

God. It's funny how something that is such a standard sentiment in times like this seems so meaningless when you are on the receiving end of the message. Looking around the room and seeing only tears and whispers of sadness, the room felt heavy and oppressive to me. As bad as it sounded, I thought God to be quite selfish if He took her so that she could be with Him while it caused this many people so much pain. I looked up at the cross in the room and whispered, "Look at how many lives she touched. Why now? I can't understand. Why aren't You answering me?" Still, no response.

After the last visitor had paid their respects, we headed home. Sleep, though deeply desired, continued to elude me. I hadn't really slept more than a couple of hours each night since it happened. I laid awake in bed, my mind whirling with activity. How would I get through this? What about when my baby was born? Mom wouldn't be there. She had heard the heartbeat mere days before she died but would never get to hold her second grandchild. That was devastating to me. My son loved his grandma and spent so much time with her. He was only two weeks away from his third birthday, and she would not be here to celebrate with him. There was only one question I continued to ask God. I yelled at God and demanded to know "Why?"

No matter how many times I asked, there was never an answer. I began to believe that God was punishing me for turning away from Him. I knew that when I was angry with someone I would ignore them until I was good and ready to have a conversation. God was obviously doing the same

Chapter 9

with me. What other explanation was there? Having grown up with the teachings of fire and brimstone, it occurred to me that I had been deemed a loss to the kingdom, and He would focus on those who would be better-suited to follow His words. That might sound crazy to you, but it was the only explanation I could think of that made any sense for His silence. I felt no sense of peace and heard no whisper of encouragement. Rest was not to come that night and I did not know it at that moment, but I would have my answer from Him the next day.

Chapter 10

Every pew was filled. Flowers were everywhere. Different shades of blue were in every floral arrangement because it was my mother's favorite color. It was evident how many people were aware of that fact. I felt a sense of calm that hadn't been there before. Peace, I guess I would call it. I thought it strange that I would feel that way but maybe it was exhaustion. We began to make our way toward the front of the church to our reserved seating, and as I walked, my eyes were fixed on both the casket and the cross. This image had been etched forever into my memory. Even now, over twenty-five years later, I can see it as clearly as I did that day. I could smell the flowers, hear the music and even remember the way the sunlight came through the windows, like walkways to Heaven that shone directly on the casket. The service began with prayers, and the songs I had previously recorded being played. That part seemed secondary. The pastor got up to speak and what he said was the one thing I have never forgotten. I believed now that it was God answering me. His answer was delivered through the pastor, but it was specifically for me, in a way

I could understand and connect with. It was the lesson in the quilt. He said:

"Teresa was a seamstress and she made many beautiful things. She would sew and stitch and what we saw on the outside was perfect by the pattern and design. What she saw on the inside was something else. You see, we are here on earth and we are looking up toward Heaven. We see the underside of the quilt and there are knots and tangles. The thread crosses over and under, and there is no design or picture that we can see. Teresa, she is sitting right next to the Father. She is looking at the most beautiful quilt and seeing a design that is exactly as it was intended to be. Our eyes see only the work in progress, but she is seeing the final design. We may not understand why, but we must take comfort that, when His design is finished, it will be exactly as He planned, and we will see the beauty in His time."

The tears came fast and furious. I remembered all the times we had sewn something together. When I would question why something was done a certain way, my mother's response was always, "That's how the pattern is designed, and when it's done it will be exactly the way it should be." It was as if I was receiving an answer and encouragement from both God and my mother. Looking back, He had answered my question many times before. I simply wasn't in a circumstance, or wasn't willing, to learn the true meaning of those answers until now. While I was sure that more than one person took comfort from those words that day, there was no one that would have pulled it as close to their heart as me. For the first time since I

Chapter 10

lost her, I slept the entire night. At home, I pulled out the old faithful quilt she had given me and I saw it with new vision. That quilt came to represent the very message of hope, love, and understanding that God had for all of us. The quilt had always provided a sense of comfort that I attached to my mother, whose loving hands had made it, but from that moment on it was so much more. It was a visible representation of her favorite phrase, "Everything happens for a reason." I didn't know it then, but that quilt would become my very tether to God, and would bring me through some rough times ahead. It would stay with me and provide the comfort and strength I needed until I was finally able to continue in faith on my own.

Chapter 11

It is often said that when we are finally starting a turnaround, Satan comes for us the hardest. He certainly has tested my faith a lot in the years since. Within days of my mother's funeral, I was tested in my marriage when I learned my husband had been spending time with another woman. I found out when the phone bill came in and saw several calls to this person, including on the day of my mother's funeral. When I asked his co-workers about it, they confirmed my suspicions. Our finances were in shambles as well, and I remember crying when I dropped a gallon of milk because I didn't have the money to buy another. My aunt was also attempting to assist in the reconciliation between my father and I.

I was helping everyone else cope, working, and due to have my second baby in a month, so I really could not deal with one more thing. I wish I could say that my faith was strong enough to turn straight to God, but it wasn't and I didn't. I thought maybe I misunderstood His message from the funeral. I mean, this was a lot of tangles and knots that didn't lead to anything beautiful. I learned in church as a youth that we all had a purpose. I decided I was God's "crash test dummy." I truly believed that maybe my purpose was to see how much one human being could take in the shortest amount of time. It sounds completely ridiculous to say that now, but I bet that at some point, you have felt the same way too.

While I was sarcastic about my purpose, I did return to prayer. Basically, I prayed to ask what I had done to deserve all of this. Don't get me wrong; I am well aware that there are people in this world who have suffered far more in life than me, and I do not discount that at all. What is minor to one person is life-changing to another, but the concepts are still the same. Yet, where you find your strength, no matter the situation, is individual. My hope is that the message of my experiences can help someone in theirs. It is fraught with twists and turns, and sometimes we stumble off the path for a time. No one guaranteed that the path would be a straight line. You can find your way back to happiness and your spiritual self. This is simply how it happened for me. My hope is that you can find at least one small thing in my story that you can build on for yours.

Chapter 12

Let me take a moment to clear up a myth about losing someone. Time does not "take away the pain," as most people say. Time doesn't heal either. What time does is help you learn how to deal with the loss and the memories. How you deal can be either good, bad, or a combination of both. The word "loss" for me was the loss of several loved ones, a marriage, finances, and more recently, the loss of a grandchild. For you, it may mean any or all of these, or something else entirely, like loss of a job, friendship, a home, etc. The process of grieving is the same regardless of the circumstance, it just may be shorter or longer in duration. I handled loss by becoming angry and sarcastic, especially toward God.

I am not afraid to admit that and I think He is pleased to have me finally acknowledge it. Every time something bad would happen, I would wrap up in that quilt, have a good cry, and ask God what I did to make Him so mad. The funny thing is that each and every time, the answer I received were the words of the pastor at the funeral that day. I would turn it upside down and see the imperfections of a tangle or knot, but try as I might, I couldn't buy into the idea that something great was going to manifest from all the hurt.

I realize I have shared a lengthy discussion of gloom and doom, but it's necessary to fully grasp where I was (and where you may be as well), so that the message of the quilt becomes real. Every time I had a problem I went straight for the quilt. I would wallow in my problems, ask God why, and then remember the words of the message. I finally realized I knew how to fix it. I started by going back to church, every Sunday, no matter what. I would sit in the pew, sing along, and bow my head while the pastor prayed. I was there and going through the motions, but I wasn't *there*. I was there as a means of negotiation, which is commonly a first step for people trying to get back in God's good grace. I thought that by showing up God would be happy with me and things would turn around.

Well things didn't turn around, and in fact, I started to feel like I was being punished even more for not being sincere. My marriage got worse, my relationships with family were strained, and I felt trapped and suffocated. Believing that God was angry at me was a coping mechanism and a way to avoid taking a hard look at myself. Many of us have been taught that God is an angry God, but that is simply untrue. God is not a punisher. He is a provider. He gave us free will and allows things to happen because of it. Just look at Jonah. He ran from God and because of that free-will decision, ended up in the belly of a giant fish. God delivered him after he truly understood the lesson, and even Jonah was angry with God at one point. He freed me too and

Chapter 12

could do the same for you. Admittedly, it took me years to finally get it, but what is amazing with God is that it's never too late. I happened to be a pretty stubborn student who was fond of figuring it out for myself.

After my marriage ended, several years and many heartbreaks later, I had my real turnaround. I moved to a new city, took a new job that paid about half of what I made before, and received little to no child support. I had no friends or family in the new town. It was me and my two children, who were teenagers at the time. That quilt went with me and got a *lot* of usage in the first year.

One day, I was home alone and feeling pretty sorry for myself. I was worried about how I was going to buy some things I knew my daughter needed for school, and how I would handle all of the living expenses for the month. I was working double shifts almost every day and I was bone-tired. The quilt was calling me so I made myself some hot chocolate and wrapped myself up in it. Music is therapy to me so I turned on the radio and tried to find a station. I scanned stations until I heard a beat I really liked. I had no idea what the station was but the music was upbeat and caught my attention, so I left it there. When the words started, I felt as if that song was played at that very moment just for me. "When the waves are taking you under, hold on just a little bit longer. He knows that this is gonna make you stronger, stronger." The song was "Stronger" by Mandisa, and it was speaking directly to me.

I began to cry, more than I had cried in a very long time, and in that moment of pure vulnerability, I knew I could not do it alone. I also realized that I wasn't alone and that I never had been. Oh, it had felt that way on plenty of occasions, but it was because I wasn't open to allowing Him to be there with me. I had been putting all my faith in my own abilities and in the physical presence of the quilt. The quilt would dry my tears, make me feel better, help me think and work out the answers. The quilt was the tangible place where my faith had been for years. Instead of running to God with my brokenness, I ran to the quilt. I saw the message from years before at my mother's funeral with a clarity I never had before. I took the quilt and turned it inside-out so that only the underside was visible. As I sat there listening to that song, I realized that it's on the "ugly" side that we can be closer than ever to God. He is there in times of trouble, but He never forces Himself upon us. I saw that I was just a tangled mess of knots that looked like it had no purpose. What I really was, and still am, is a beautiful work of art that is still in progress. You are too, and that's okay.

You may think I had some big and elaborate revelation scene like in a movie, but in fact, it was quiet and small. More than anything it was a moment of total vulnerability. With tears flowing, I simply said out loud, "I cannot do this alone and I am tired of trying to. God, I need your help."

I had never felt more of a moment of peace in my life as I did when I said those words. For the first time in almost two years, I felt that I could breathe. I didn't know how, but I felt a calming presence that told me everything was going to be okay and that I could rest now. When I said

Chapter 12

rest, I really meant it. I fell asleep on the couch and slept for over twelve hours, which was probably more than I had slept in the past month. I was still wrapped in the quilt when I woke up, but this time it had a whole new meaning. From that moment on, I took the lesson of the quilt and really internalized it. It became, and still is, the single most important message I live by. That message is simply: God sees the outcome while I only see the mess.

Part 2
Lessons from a Quilt

Chapter 13

Up to now, I have shared my struggle with faith and trusting God through the loss of my mother. I have mentioned the issues within my marriage. I did not delve into details with that part of my life because I wished to protect those involved, and also because I have forgiven. Forgiveness is important to your own healing. I had to forgive others, myself, and in my heart, even God. There have been many moments since where I had to put the lessons of the quilt into practice. I even used the same phrase I hated so much as a young girl, "Everything happens for a reason," with my own children.

Here is what I know for sure: Every time I tried to handle things on my own and without God, only tears, frustration, and struggle followed. After that moment on the couch when I was at my weakest and humbly asked for help, things took a turnaround. From that moment forward, I actually used the quilt upside down as a visual reminder that He was taking those tangles and making something amazing. In time, the quilt became tattered and torn. Eventually, it was set aside as I realized I no longer needed the physical manifestation of the lessons it provided. The meaning and lesson is with me all the time. Even now, when I am in a situation where I am searching for answers, guidance or merely a chance to vent to God, that quilt becomes a vivid picture in my mind. Now, I am giving that gift to you. A quilt of lessons that you can use to help you move forward through times of struggle. With this gift, I cannot guarantee that things will always be easy. I have suffered frustrations, worry, and heartbreaking loss, and feel certain I will do so in the future. It does not mean that God is angry with me or doesn't love me. It means that this is a time of trial, and with faith and these lessons, I can see God do amazing things.

Chapter 14

Lesson #1:
Everything Happens for a Reason

Let's get the hardest one to accept out of the way first. Throughout my life, this sentence frustrated me. It irritated me. Sometimes, it downright made me angry. When you are in a situation that is less than desirable or causing you significant pain, the last thing you really want to hear is that you are there for a reason. I drove myself crazy trying to figure out the reason so I completely understand. So why is this the first lesson? Because it's true. Before you get upset and stop reading (which I probably would have done before too) hear me out. Be forewarned that you may get a little frustrated or even angry with me, especially if you are in the throes of a bad situation. Don't give up and stop reading. You have made it this far. What comes next may be the one simple thing you need to hear to help change your thinking and put your life on a completely different path.

The first thing people say in hard situations, especially the most horrific, is that God can't be real or He is an angry God who is punishing you. I always preferred the punishment theory. The first thing I had to realize is that God gave us free will. He loved us enough to give us the ability to choose. Adam and Eve are the first examples of free will. They chose to eat the apple even though they knew it was wrong. Do not misinterpret what I am saying here. I do not mean that every bad thing that happens is because of your own free will. What I am saying is that one choice made in free will can create a wormhole of circumstances. It's like a domino effect and when you find yourself making decisions on the lesser of two evils, you are in the vortex of free will. You can free yourself of this using *trust* and one simple phrase – "Not my will, but Yours be done." It may not feel like it now, but God wants good things for you. The key is that you have to trust and wait on Him. He can take the worst of circumstances and use them for good, but you must trust in His timing and His plan.

It's almost impossible to just wake up tomorrow and follow this idea 100% of the time, so do what I did and take it one situation at a time. I started with my finances. I was getting no child support and working lots of overtime, but had no idea how I would feed us, much less pay the rent. I decided that since I wasn't brave enough to give all my problems to Him, I would go in baby steps. I crawled before I walked. I saw Him provide almost immediately when only three days later I received a refund check in the mail from my insurance for overpayment. I was able to cover the school expenses for my daughter and buy groceries. We even had a little left over. Not long after,

Chapter 14

He provided a better position at work (and did so several times in subsequent years) that allowed me to make what I needed to support us. I was able to start a savings account, rebuild my credit, buy a car, a townhome, pay for college for myself in cash, and, at under age fifty, be debt free. This did not come all at once and I am absolutely not rich, but the principle of trust has proven Him true over and over. What I found, and you will too, is that He will show you time after time that He is your provider. The more you trust Him, the more you will be able to see past the problems and into the ways He takes care of you. You see, the reason that sometimes things happen to us is because He wants to show you how much He loves you and wants to provide for you. The key is to give Him the trust that allows it to happen. As I continue to tithe and give back to others as well, I see a constant supply to cover my needs. I have also found that by starting with one simple area of your life and seeing His good work, you will begin to build your faith muscles. It's like when you work out and you add weight or repetitions as your body gets stronger; in time, you find yourself giving up more and more control to His great love for you.

You may be in a situation that is much harder. You are not there by your own free will. How does this still apply? I've been there too. My marriage was toxic and difficult. I did not connect this lesson until a couple of years after the relationship ended, but now I see that God had a perfect partner for me. Maybe if I had not gone through the things I did in my marriage, I would not be able to fully appreciate the goodness of God when He sent my current husband into my life. In the natural world, it would never seem feasible that we would have ever found each other. Our story was full of what most people called coincidences, but we knew that it was God. With God, there are no coincidences. He worked out the tangles of my past relationship to ready me for the beautiful and loving one I have now. He put every piece into place to bring us together, and in the timing that was right according to His plan.

One of the most difficult things I have ever had to deal with was the loss of our first grandchild. I never even got to hold her. My son and his fiancé were expecting, and all of us thought things were going well in the pregnancy. Her checkups were all good and we were anxious to meet Amee Jayde.

At that time, my husband and I were working two weeks a month on a cruise ship, and so I had gotten a message from my son to call him when I could one day, while we were sailing. I went to the office and called home. He said he was taking her to the hospital because they thought it was time. I told my husband and we were on cloud nine. A little while later, I got another message to call my son as soon as possible. I ran downstairs, excited to hear all about our beautiful granddaughter. What I got when he answered the phone was crying and screaming to the point that I couldn't understand what was being said. All I heard was, "We lost her. She's gone."

I didn't believe I was comprehending, but I got him to calm down enough to tell me what was happening. Amee

Chapter 14

Jayde was gone. She didn't make it. It turned out there was a very large cyst that had appeared and grown so quickly that it was pressing against the baby. It was a rare form of issue that we did not even know existed. The pressure of it killed our sweet little girl. His fiancé had to have emergency surgery to remove it. There were absolutely no words that I could write here that could describe what I was feeling. First, I was in the middle of the ocean, with no way to get home for another two days. Second, my own child was suffering the most difficult pain that any parent could ever go through and I could not fix it. Third, I was also grieving the loss of my first grandchild, named after me. Here is the interesting twist. When I got back to shore and went straight to the hospital, both my son and his fiancé were there. They explained that Amee Jayde had lost her life but had saved the life of her mother. Had that cyst burst, they both would have died. My own son looked at me and said, "Everything happens for a reason. We are heartbroken and sad, but Amee Jayde is an angel. She saved her mom's life. We are thankful for that."

Honestly, I didn't want to hear that particular statement and if you have experienced a similar thing, you don't either. What I do know is that God had a reason. He used Amee Jayde to save one life instead of losing two. I would be untruthful if I said I still don't have moments where I am sad and think of what she might have looked like or the adventures we may have shared with her. We called her "Bug," and each time I see a ladybug I think of her. I also thank God that we still have her mother in our lives, as she has been a blessing for my son and all of us. The key takeaway is this: Whatever you are going through, know that God is using it for good. He is either blessing you, teaching you, molding you, and in some cases, saving you.

Chapter 15

Lesson #2:
Be Careful Where You Put Your Faith

It is very easy to put your faith and trust in people and things because we can physically see them. Sometimes they pull through for us, but more often than not, they let us down. Over time, we can place too much emphasis on trying to find answers, happiness, peace or acceptance in these people and things. That can lead to a path of heartbreak, tough roads, and even destruction. Remember the free will we spoke of? It lives in this area in a very tangible way. We begin to see our worth through the eyes of others. We wrap ourselves in the quilt of our jobs, finances, and relationships. These can even begin to replace more important things like family and faith. Having a career path is a wonderful thing, but the more you put your faith and self-worth into your position, the more that career takes over and becomes an "idol."

I can speak from experience that it is very easy to be grateful to God when everything is going wonderfully, but the first thing I did when times got rough was believe He was angry at me. At one time, I had the biggest house on the block, cars, jewelry, trips, and money in the bank. I also had a lot of debt and stress to go with it. My ex-husband was very much about *Keeping Up with the Joneses*, and I was drowning. When I did look at all we had, I very much gave myself the credit. I got that promotion, I worked hard, and was rewarded. The promise of the next career step and all that came with it became the goal. The focus was on what's next or what more I could achieve. When I lost it all, I had to come to grips with the reality that lifestyle was the idol. I could count on one hand how many times I stopped to thank God for His blessings during that phase in my life. I had not yet had that vulnerable moment. I was angry all the time, in a bad marriage, and still grieving my mother and others I had lost. I took credit for the things He saw fit to bless me with because He loved me.

My mother used to use the quote, "The Lord giveth and the Lord taketh away." It is a true statement and I have had to learn that lesson more than once in life. I am a bit stubborn I suppose. Sometimes, it isn't because we have another idol. Sometimes, it is because He has something much better for us, but we are so comfortable where we are that we are unwilling to move toward it ourselves. Short version: He gives us a kick in the pants! He will never close a door without opening another one, but we have to be willing to trust in His plan. Admittedly, this has also been extremely difficult for me to do because I am a planner. I like to know what to expect. I have a vision of what things

Chapter 15

are supposed to look like. Like the quilt, so many things were a comfort to me, because I knew exactly what to expect. My mother was the largest one of these things. We all have a purpose and when God took her, it was because He needed her for something else. I also believe it was to push me from under her wing to become the person I am today. He wasn't punishing me by taking her; He was opening a door for me to stand on my own two feet and become the person of faith and strength I am today.

It's okay to have trust and faith in people, I am not telling you to be distrusting at all. Just have the understanding that God has placed them in your life for a reason. Some are to help us along in the plan that He has for us. Others are to challenge us to overcome or learn a lesson. Still more are intended to cause us to surrender it all to Him and watch Him provide, protect, and work in ways that no mortal thing could ever do. It is this last one that is the largest and hardest, but which is also the most rewarding. I learned this lesson in a big way over the past couple of years.

I needed a job change and had applied and interviewed for three different jobs. I did not get any of them and was extremely frustrated. I was praying for guidance, but secretly hoping that I would get my way and get one of them. By the way, there is no such thing as having secrets from God. He knew my intentions. One day on my daily run, I said, "Okay Lord, I don't know what the deal is, but I am driving myself crazy trying to figure this job thing out. I am tired of getting my hopes up only to be let down. What's the deal?" (Side note: This is literally how I talk to God: like

He is running beside me. There is no right way to pray - only your way.) Then Covid hit and everything stopped. When businesses reopened, I was one of the first people called back to work. My job had drastically changed, but I had a job. God provided. Also, those other jobs that I was so upset I didn't get... they were eliminated. God also protected. You see He had a plan for me way before I even knew all of this would happen. I had put my faith in my work ethic and experience, and the promises of people at work; yet, they all failed me. God, however, did not. He protected and provided for me in a time when no else could.

For the next year, I worked the job He had provided, but I was praying desperately for something else. I had lost a lot of trust in the leadership of where I worked, as they had misled me when they called me back. I had gone ten years backward in my career. I thanked Him every day for the job, and for taking care of me, and I did the job to the best of my ability. I did not slack off or call out all the time. I prayed every single day for guidance on a new opportunity and trusted that God had a plan. It turned out that after a year, an opportunity pretty much found me, and not only did He line up the timing perfectly, but He also restored me to my pre-Covid situation. I could work from home, my income would go up, and my work hours would still coincide with my husband, and my service with the Worship team at my church. No one but God has that sort of perfect planning, and I continue to be grateful for it. He truly showed me in a big way that by giving my situation over to Him, I would be amazed.

Chapter 15

It is not easy to do this, but I promise you it will be worth it in ways you cannot imagine. It is human emotion that prevents us from being able to take this step, but just start simple. Pick one thing and put it completely in His hands. Write it down and put it away. Once sealed, it is gone from your hands and given to His. Pray over it. Really and truly turn the outcome over to Him. Understand, the result may not be what you want, but trust that it is what you need. There is a plan for you and it may be years before you see it. You may never truly understand why He works it out the way He does, but other seeds of greatness can grow from it. Put your faith and trust in the right hands... His hands. Let Him guide you in your fears, doubts, and struggles. Let Him wrap you in His love, grace, and mercy. It is more comforting than any quilt could ever be, and better... it will never wear out!

Chapter 16

Lesson #3:
Ugly Can Become Beautiful

As you walk through the castle at Walt Disney World, you are surrounded by beautiful mosaics. These pictures tell the story of Cinderella in stunning color and detail. Taking over twenty-two months to create and containing around 300,000 tiles, they are truly a sight to behold. Think about that for a moment. There are 300,000 tiles, and each one was individually placed exactly where it needed to be to complete the picture. What we see now is the finished product. Before completion, however, it was all only piles of tiles and dust. To everyone but the artists, it was an ugly pile of debris. The same can be said for our situations in life sometimes. We find ourselves standing in the middle of what appears to be the shattered glass of our lives, hopes, and dreams. All around us is dirt, ugliness, and shards of situations that we cannot see a reason or a purpose for. Like the artists who created the Cinderella castle mosaic, God takes all of those random pieces and creates a new work of art in you. Artists use the available items around them to turn what some see as trash or leftover pieces into amazing works that command attention and renown. No two art pieces are exactly the same, and neither are we. Each of us has our own story, our own victories and defeats. If you can give God the ability to use it, He will take every single piece of what is left and create the mosaic of your life.

Everyone is familiar with pottery and how it is made. That ugly, wet clump of clay goes onto a wheel and begins to spin at various rates of speed. At the highest speed, the shape begins to form, and during the slower speeds, the detail starts to evolve. Sometimes the potter sees something emerging that is not part of the design plan. When that happens, the potter will collapse the entire piece, only to start again. The potter sees the final image and what the ultimate design of the piece will be. To the untrained viewer, we think that what they had begun to create seemed good enough. To the artist, that piece of clay is destined for greater designs. The same is true of us with God. We may see that what we have looks good enough, but God sees the final design as only a Creator can. He takes us and molds us with gentle and loving hands until we become that one of a kind creation that no one else can replicate.

Like the pastor said at my mother's funeral that day, the quilt is a beautiful tapestry of odd scraps and pieces of fabric. It contains the leftovers, the unused, and unwanted pieces. My mother saw a purpose in those pieces. She saw a design that was only visible to her until it was completed. You may feel the same as one of those pieces of fabric. You may feel cast aside and unwanted by someone you cared about deeply. You may feel overlooked and unappreciated for your sacrifices in your job. You may feel lost and forgotten like a piece of fabric in the bottom of a basket. Whatever you are feeling, give it to God. Trust that, like that mosaic or the quilt, there is beauty in the remnants of things destroyed. In my mother's quilt, the original fabric created a dress or shirt, but it was the castoff pieces that created a treasured item that provided comfort, warmth, and safety for years. The broken pieces, once put back together into something new and beautiful, remained long after the original articles were gone or forgotten. There is beauty in the brokenness of our lives. Strength that comes from walking in the faith that God is working on putting all of those pieces together into the quilt of our lives. Hope comes when you wrap yourself in that promise and trust that He has great things for you. It's uncomfortable to have to wait, but there isn't a single masterpiece of art in the world today that was created overnight. Michelangelo took over two years to create "David." It took him four years to paint the Sistine Chapel. Even a beautiful garden takes time to provide beautiful flowers that sprout from dark and ugly seeds.

As I moved back into a relationship with God, I began to find that what I saw as an ugly and tattered life was really the foundation of something truly beautiful. I started by putting my trust in Him with my finances and grew from there. It took hard work and discipline on my part because great things do not come without effort, but His provision never failed me. When I didn't see a way, one always appeared in the form of a raise, a new job opportunity, an unexpected refund, etc. He took the broken pieces of the relationship with my father and created a new one that I cherish. Within a week of my mother's passing, my father and I had dinner together and talked. We began to try and put the pieces of the past behind us and move toward a new time in our relationship. Only recently did we both realize that we did not know that each of us felt the same way – hurt, forgotten, unaware. It has been small steps and there have been tears and laughter. I often wonder if my mother had not passed away at that particular point in my life, if he and I would ever have reconciled. I will never know all the circumstances that affected our relationship, but I am grateful that God has given us the time to try and move forward.

God also took the shattered glass of my tender heart and brought me a person to love, who would, through God, put it back together and make it better than before. My new husband has been able to help me build my faith, achieve my own goals (such as this book), and see love for what it should be. God knew exactly the person I, and my children, needed in our lives to put the mosaic back together. I could never have imagined the life and love I experience every day with my husband. I didn't even think I deserved it but God designed beauty from the ashes of my relationship scars. God takes the ugly and makes it beautiful. There is hope in that for all of us.

Chapter 17

Lesson #4:
God Answers in Ways We Don't Always Recognize and in His Timing

Have you ever heard someone say that God spoke to them? I have heard it a lot in my life, and I always wondered why He never spoke to me. I would ask Him questions, like when my mother died or my marriage failed, but never heard any booming voice from the Heavens answer me. Only recently did I come to understand that God had been answering me for years, but I didn't recognize it as Him. Because we are all different, He reaches us in the way that is meant only for us. I fully believe that He speaks in a literal voice to some people. To others, it may be a whisper, the roar of the ocean, a gut feeling, or all of the above. I often joke that God pretty much gives me "billboards," because He has been telling me all along, but I need to be hit in the face with it to finally grasp it.

Children are full of innocence and simple understanding. While adults complicate and overanalyze things, children can see the same situation with the simplest of solutions. Think of how many times a young person has helped you with something technology related in one or two clicks! God uses children to speak to us sometimes and He definitely did for me. My son was about to turn three when my mother died. Only three weeks after her funeral, I found myself making cupcakes for his daycare to celebrate his birthday. Something as simple as putting sprinkles on top completely overwhelmed me and I could not seem to get it to work. I went to the bathroom where I sat at the edge of the sink and cried. My son came in and took my hands. He said, "Are you sad mommy?"

"Yes," I said.

"Are you sad that your mommy is gone?"

"Yes, and I don't know how to get the sprinkles on your cupcakes for school."

"Take my hand, Mommy, and I will help you. We can do it together. I'm here with you."

My son is now almost thirty, and this was one moment of our lives that I have never, and will never, forget. He took my hand and walked me back to the kitchen. He picked up a cupcake, turned it upside down, and dipped it in the bowl of sprinkles. Looking up at me and smiling, he simply said, "See. It will be okay."

I didn't see it then, but in the many years since, when I think back on that single moment, I realize that God was there. He was there in the words of my son, telling me that He was with me and that He would help me get through. I don't know if I have ever shared with my son how much that moment has meant to me, but I know I should. It was in the words and the voice of a child, but with all the love and grace of our heavenly Father.

God knows best how to reach us, but we have to be willing to hear Him. I know unequivocally that He was speaking to me through the pastor at my mother's funeral. He was answering the questions and giving me an explanation that I probably didn't deserve. I have come to recognize that God talks to me a lot more than I think. He does it through other people, through situations, and even through my gut feelings.

I had a job opportunity a couple of years ago and was on the third round of interviews. The next day I was running and thinking about the job. I often talk to God as I run because it is my quiet time. Sometimes, it also involves praying that I can actually finish the run I am doing - it's hot in Florida in the summer! I had this uneasy feeling about the job and whether it would be right to take it if offered. As usual, I was trying to figure it all out in my head, running through the pay (which would be a cut), schedule, etc., and how it would affect my current life situation. No matter what, I could not shake the odd feeling I had about it. It was a feeling I couldn't identify, other than to say it didn't feel right. This is something that I tend to have regularly when I am about to make a change. If I feel at peace with something, then the change has always worked out for me. If I don't and do it anyway, it's a disaster. I passed on the job and good thing I did, because Covid happened and the entire business was shut down! I would have been unemployed.

Instead, I stayed where I was, and as I mentioned earlier, remained employed and with income during the entire pandemic until a better opportunity was provided to me.

Even things can be a form of communication. The symbol of this book is the quilt and that is the absolute best example I have from my life on how He talked to me. He took the words of the pastor, which fused onto the visual and tangible item and put the message on my heart forever. It is still the single most referenced moment with God I have experienced. That message carries me through when life isn't going the way I had hoped, or when I find myself feeling like maybe things won't work out. We all have things that remind us of our weakest and strongest moments in life. These things are visual reminders of how God can reach us no matter where we are. Quite simply, He can use anything to do a work in our lives. A piece of jewelry, a book, a song, a feeling, or any number of things are all ways that He reaches us. We only have to be open and willing to listen and to accept the message. Sometimes, He tells us that everything is going to work out. Sometimes, He tells us that what we want is not what is meant for us to have. Sometimes, He is calling you to something higher. Whatever it is, He knows your purpose and He knows your best form of communication. He created you and will use whatever is necessary to show His love for you and give you peace and hope.

Chapter 18

There is no way that I could ever have imagined that my life could be this happy and full of love before. God knew. He always knew. Just like the artist, He had a vision for me which culminated in this book. I have one goal for this book. It is very simply to help merely one person. If that one person can find a new way to move through any loss by building a relationship with God, then it has all been worth it. The moments of self-doubt, fear, anguish, and hope will matter to someone.

I resisted the idea to write a book for years because I felt that I didn't have anything worth sharing. How could I possibly help anyone when I struggle with these things myself? God helped me to see that my struggle is entirely the point. Maybe the way He will reach someone is through my words, like He reaches me so often. I will be the first to say that I still have moments of frustration or feel like maybe I'm being punished. Every time I do, I look at a picture of a quilt and am quickly reminded that the situation is just one piece of a beautiful picture.

You are too. You are one of millions of pieces of God's picture for the world. You have greatness inside of you, if you are only willing to put your trust in the Artist. Take the ugly and that which you do not understand, give it to Him, and watch Him make something beautiful. Surrender your life and your outcomes to Him and watch the masterpiece emerge. Find a visual reminder and place it where you will see it daily. It may be a mosaic coaster, a picture of a piece of art you love, or even a quilt. Better yet, make one! You will then be able to see it for the work and struggle it takes to create what you will see in the finished product. Know that you are something beautiful and that your struggles are but one part of what makes you one of a kind. Your struggle can be the springboard for not only yourself, but others to reach full potential. You can offer this world something that no one else can...YOU. Take every situation and look for the beauty in it or the lesson that can be learned. It isn't easy, but it is worth it. Do not let fear, doubt, insecurity, loss or anger take you away from the beautiful outcome God has for you.

Acknowledgements

I would be remiss if I did not offer gratitude to those who have helped me as I made the trek from idea to completion of this book. First and foremost, to God, who kept tugging at my heart to write it. He knows the purpose behind it and will guide this book to the people who need it most. My husband, Alan, who supports me in every goal and crazy dream I come up with. Thank you for pushing me to hit the "submit" button and get past my fears. To my children, Joey and Teesha – you have always seen me as so much more than I ever saw myself. There have been many times when you have taught me just as much as I taught you. Thank you to Kelsi, who helped me to connect with the publishing group. Finally, to all of those in the publishing area that spent time with me, encouraged me, prayed with me, and answered my sometimes ridiculous questions... thank you. Writing a book is a lonely project, but I never truly felt alone!

CPSIA information can be obtained
at www.ICGtesting.com
Printed in the USA
BVHW040258200122
626621BV00014B/1432